OLUFEMI OGUNBANWO

What about Community?

Living the way God designed

All Bible quotations are from the New American Standard Version (NASB) 1995 edition, except where otherwise stated.

First edition

This book was professionally typeset on Reedsy.
Find out more at reedsy.com

This work is dedicated to
My dear wife and children, my primary community; without you, I am simply wandering.
My beloved Love Ward peoples of aged fellowship; you stirred the first longings and provided the initial joys of community.
My encouragers and challengers (you know yourselves); without your fellowship I probably would never have written this work.
To all who long for more than casual church relationships and those who suspect that there must be more; may you find some answers here.

Contents

Foreword

Thomas W Bowden
(New Covenant Community. Greenwich, NY)

Having been a part of a Christian community for over forty years, I am blessed by Olufemi's desire to embrace this form of church structure and share his burden for community with others. I feel compelled to remind the reader that this is not a book about advocacy nor is it about political or social activism. Though these may be well-intended they are of a completely different origin and nature than that of a Christian community. The former is built on the strength, wisdom, and righteousness of men while the latter is built on the grace, wisdom, and righteousness of God. At times they may look alike and sound alike, but they are not from the same spirit. Reformers believe they can change world systems which is something Jesus never did nor commissioned His Church to do. We are the called out ones who are building the spiritual kingdom of God and its citizenship on the earth.

Few Christians have ever given much thought to the topic of church structure. This is not exactly where one would think to turn when in need of spiritual inspiration, strengthened faith, or renewed hope but God's order for His Church does supply these things in good measure.

This book challenges us to consider the possibility that many of our spiritual and natural frustrations may be the result of trying to live for God with our whole hearts within a church structure that may also be frustrating the grace of God. Men will defend their institutions with passion but must ask themselves whether contemporary church structure was God's intention from the beginning or something church leaders unwittingly carried with them while climbing out of the Dark Ages.

As you read, you will see that the Lord has placed so many right desires in the hearts of so many people who find themselves frustrated by human institutions while attempting to fulfil those desires. For the Holy Ghost filled believers in Jesus Christ, these desires will become a spiritual burden: to be a contributing part of a people committed to the fulfilment of God's purposes unto His glory. It is toward such hearts as these that this book is written.

The accounts and testimonies in this book are from men who have come to the end of what many call "church." Being led by the Holy Ghost throughout the centuries, men and women have come to understand that churches were not intended to be religious organizations but living organisms providing all that is necessary for life and godliness. There may be good churches functioning in a wrong framework, but now the Spirit is quickening hearts to recognize the order He has ordained as revealed in both the Old and New Testaments and is testified to in this book.

The references to the Christian community recorded here are from centuries past to the present day. All Christian communities do not follow one singular model. Each community will have its diversities though the same spiritual principles precipitated their beginnings and define their purpose. The men who began these communities also are personally diverse yet have been drawn to the vision of community by the same burdens and scriptural revelations.

I have a special appreciation for the chapter that outlines the rules and guidelines that are required to keep harmony and order in any community. Without these, men will do what is right in their own eyes and there will be no true unity. The spiritual sanity and sensibility of these guidelines testify to the safety and health that abide within the community.

Olufemi's use of Paul's metaphor of the human body representing the Church will challenge the reader to consider the extent to which he is fulfilling these scriptures. Most secular organizations could also use the human body as an example of their structure. In like manner, conventional church systems can do the same, but it is in the context of a Spirit-filled community that the metaphor of the human body takes on a deeper and richer application.

We are living in a day when God-given words of substance, such as family and community, are used much too quickly, easily, cheaply, and often. Marketers often use the words family and community to appeal to our God-given need for both. We are not a family nor are we a community simply because we have purchased the same items as others or belong to the same organizations. Using words of substance for something does not automatically give those things substance. This is not so when we speak of Christian community. Jesus Christ is the only name by which the family in heaven and on earth is named.

This book ends with the story of a utopian city where everyone is so in love with the Lord that the presence of money or the need for it is alien. By no means is this suggesting that Christian community is a moneyless spiritual order. I believe the purpose of this story is to quicken people's hearts to the fact that their values can transcend those of self-promotion, status, covetousness, or any other form of selfishness.

We all know that when Jesus comes and tears down the kingdoms of this world, He will then establish His own Kingdom and His glory will fill the whole earth. The whole earth will be one united and holy community where everyone will be of one mind and spirit. Until that day comes, we need to reach as high as we can for as much of that kingdom as we can, ushering in the Day of the Lord. My hope is that this book will have its small part toward that end.

Reviews

Carlton B Williams, Th.D
(Founder High Life World. Lagos Nigeria)

We live in unique times. Paul the Apostle emphasized to his early listeners that we are those 'upon whom the ends of the ages have come'[1] . The Lord promised through His prophets that despite the deepening fragmentation and darkness we will experience in the world during these end days, divine models will be revealed through His people; not for the sake of exclusivity or to increase reclusivity, but to educate humanity into the rediscovery of paths that lead to true peace and harmony.

In this short book, Femi reveals such a path. As technology-induced social isolation has now given way to fear-induced actual isolation, heaven shows the way forward: community. Rather than social distancing, heaven points to integration. Though counterculture, we are helped to remember that as part of His prayer to the Father at Gethsemane, the Lord gives the glory He had received from the Father to the church for the achievement of this very purpose: that we will be one, as He and the Father are One.

---

[1]   1Cor.10:11

The oneness of the Body holds the secret to the release of the greatest expression of the Father's nature and power that the earth has ever seen. Vibrant, deep, life-giving, community-living is an essential catalyst to this oneness.

Femi provides a clear, compelling theological framework for this and examines living examples past and present that fill us with hope for the future. These are not a people that bury their heads in the sand waiting to be airlifted out of a world they are fearful of and feel ill-equipped to engage with; on the contrary, we see a people bold enough to identify what they stand for and harness the power of shared values to strengthen and deepen their beliefs, pass an unadulterated legacy to their progeny and develop a potent strategy to change the world around them.

I have seen Femi stretch towards, seek and carry this vision for many years. I highly commend this book to you and encourage that with an open heart, we allow the Lord to lead us down a path that though may be unfamiliar and seem uncomfortable, holds the key to our peace, prosperity and impact, as a new glorious day for the church dawns!

Dr Kenny Adeshugba
Charis Christian Centre, London.

Having read this book I have to concur that this is not only a book but a manual for community living. Hard though the contents may seem, it could easily set the tone for a present-day dialogue, or a futuristic model of living; the contents of the pages of this book can be a reality in many places of the world.

Historically, the African community had a framework that was built on the principles outlined by Femi. However, as civilisation and individuality set in, the fabric of communal spirit that bonds people together and gave them a common goal and purpose diminished. The model in this book is however inspired by the Book of Acts, where this was established and practised by the Christian community; hence they became the envy of others and a multitude of people desiring to join the Christians. It is the same connectedness and communal unity that brought the baptism of the Holy Spirit where they were all gathered in one accord. Femi establishes that when such spirit is in action in community, families will become stronger, the gospel will create a christocentric environment, and we will experience eradication of poverty.

This book emphasizes the importance of relationship and community; it encourages communal responsibility, and its benefits are communal financial prosperity, family solidification, ethnic connectivity and hospitality. It promotes a powerful sense of a common goal and purpose leading to making the world a better place.

Prof. Akindotun Merino
(CEO, Jars Education Group, LLC)

Pastor Femi Ogunbanwo has presented a gift to the church, an unveiling of the divine mind regarding communities. This book adds to the body of knowledge and re-ignites believers' hearts everywhere. According to Femi, communities were ordained by God for fellowship and service.

As a trained family psychologist, I am especially interested in systems. Communities are systems in which each system in connection with the other systems develop identities. Systems are interdependent and interrelated. Faulty systems can wound while healthy systems are healing and restorative.

Are we really okay with living separately and disparagingly? Is the goal of church to simply be involved in activities only to return to lonely homes? The fear of this type of message is rooted in trauma. However, we should know that we become wounded in the context of relationships but it's also within healthy relationships that we are healed.

Pastor Ogunbanwo has provided a blueprint for this type of engagement. He has evaluated failed and successful communities to present a well-researched and documented paper. The goal is so we can proceed without fear or trepidation. He addressed the fear of cults and other failed communities. We can't allow the failures of the past to keep us from living the heart of freedom. I encourage you to read this book with an open heart and let us together march forward to the promised land. These communities could become lasting legacies of the 21st-century church on earth if the Lord tarries. Who knows what we can create? We must not forget that almost all movements in history were engineered within communities. The church could definitely replicate the kingdom on earth.

Some might say, "but I attend church and have no need to belong to a Christian community." My response is why do we feel more comfortable living in secular communities instead of Christian ones? Think about it, we live in estates and neighbourhoods that were constructed to align with visions of cities and states. Minimally, these homes proceed from the owners' vision. God's vision is for thriving Christian communities. We can no longer cede ground, we can do better. We can heal from the fear of past generations and adopt this call to action.

I celebrate Femi for birthing this book, by reading it you've become an arbiter of the vision. Let's declare it far and wide. It's time to create new pathways for ourselves and future generations. Shalom.

1

Prelude

"He works on us in all sorts of ways. But above all, he works on us through each other. Men are mirrors, or "carriers" of Christ to other men. Usually it is those who know Him that bring Him to others. That is why the church, the whole body of Christians showing Him to one another, is so important. "[2] - C.S. Lewis

"The Christian life defends the single personality from the collective, not by isolating him but by giving him the status of an organ in a mystical body. As the Book of Revelation says, he is made "a pillar in the temple of God"; and it adds, "he shall go no more out" ....as mere biological entities, each with its separate will to live and to expand, we are apparently of no account; we are cross-fodder. But as organs in the Body of Christ, as stones and pillars in the temple, we are assured of our eternal self-identity and shall live to remember the galaxies as an old

---

[2]   C.S. Lewis. *Mere Christianity*. Geoffrey Bles. 1952

tale."[3] – C.S.Lewis

"It may seem strange that such an insignificant group could experience such lofty feelings of peace and community, but it was so. It was a gift from God. And only one antipathy was bound up in our love – a rejection of the systems of civilization; a hatred of the falsities of social stratification; an antagonism to the spirit of impurity; an opposition to the moral coercion of the clergy. The fight that we took up was a fight against these alien spirits. It was a fight for the spirit of God and Jesus Christ." (Eberhard Arnord, on the early stage of the Bruderhof) [4]

"Community is simply the marriage of practicality and spirituality in a structure that re-channels our natural resources of time, energy, and money in a more fruitful manner, and our spiritual resources into the framework of a more pliable wineskin." (Pastor Tom Bowden - New Covenant Community, Greenwich NY)

"The way God designed our bodies is a model for understanding our lives together as a church..... " (1Cor12:25 MSG)

"For his body has been formed in his image and is closely joined together and constantly connected as one." (Ephe4:16 The Passion Translation - TPT)

---

[3] C.S.Lewis. *Membership (an essay)*. 1945

[4] Eberhard Arnold: Writings Selected with an Introduction (edited by - Johann Christopher Arnold): Plough Publishing House, 2000.

2

Introduction

God tends to work through communities.

Right from creation God made two humans to live together, because "it is not good for man to live alone", commanding and blessing them to multiply and be productive; thus forming the earliest human community.

Marriage is a community.

Family is a community.

Skip a few generations, and we see that the promise to Abraham was not just to him but to his descendants; a formidable and ultimately universal community.

Jacob was but a man, yet Israel became a nation; a mega community with common values, religion, destiny, all dwelling on the same land.

Society is a community.

Man is a community of spirit, soul & body[5]; and the physical body is itself a community.

And as the human body, the Church (the Body of Christ) is a community; it is a mystical and universal community of local and regional communities.

I appreciate that the thought of community-living triggers all kinds of resistance in many, if not most Christians, yet I am convinced that it is God's design that his elect, the church, should live in communities. Not the virtual communities enabled by technology (as useful as that may be), nor congregations that travel from various distances for meetings (as faithful as that be), but rather intentional, land/location-sharing, covenant based, Holy Spirit inspired, Jesus glorifying, 'city on a hill' type communities; where practically all of your residential neighbours are of the same faith and intentionally pursuing the same vision and mission.

I am aware that many churches and groups are already practising community principles and lifestyle to some lesser or greater degree; ranging from regular love feasts, strategic provision for needy brethren, neighbourhood house groups, house churches, to very exemplary intentional communities that incorporate all the attributes of the listed expressions. I salute all such

---

[5] 1Thess5:23 (TPT) Now, may the God of peace and harmony set you apart, making you completely holy. And may *your entire being—spirit, soul, and body*—be kept completely flawless in the appearing of our Lord Jesus, the Anointed One.

efforts and pray that they keep growing towards the ultimate expression of body-community.

Over the next few pages, I hope to inform, encourage, inspire, motivate and challenge you about and towards this absolutely beautiful idea. I hope you enjoy the read and I also pray that you will receive revelatory power and courage to embark on this journey of a deeply enriched and enriching life.

3

Community of the human body

T he human body is made up of so many different parts. Some parts of the body will never have direct contact with each other, yet are vital to the healthy and proper function of each other, and the achievement of the design of each part. No matter how significant any part is, it is only because of what it is a part of.

If any part fails or breaks, the whole body will feel the pain and or loss, in some visceral and debilitating ways; from toothache to a broken toe, to a throat infection, to renal failure, to cancer of any kind.

Although a person may survive without some parts, the missing parts are usually due to some disease or accident or some aberration in the genetic code. The ordinary or ideal human being possesses a definite number of parts that combine for the most efficient, productive and fulfilling living.

The human, as an integrated being, is ever seeking to achieve goals of expression (I want to be known), interaction (I want to participate), education (I want to know), productivity (I want to achieve), improvement (I want to be better), preservation (I want to keep existing), and procreation (I want more of me to exist) etc. Every single part of the body, though and however unique, is ultimately only useful to the extent that it serves these common goals of the body. Even the very vital heart or liver is only useful as part of the body. If for whatever reason, any part begins to act contrary to any of these goals, it diminishes the body's being and will need to be realigned to the rest of the body (healing & repair) or disconnected from the body (removal or amputation). If any part is severed it needs urgent re-grafting, else it will wither and die.

The human body is a magnificent community of a multitude of and diverse range of parts that 'dwell' together, physically connected, sharing the same life carrying blood system and nervous system. When all is well, it works in perfect harmony, each part instinctively responding to, complementing and compensating for the others. This community of parts strives for common objectives all the time. It is a fully integrated organic community of specialized parts that are only as effective as they aid each other and the whole organism.

As the human body, so is the body of Christ, the Church.

4

Community of the Body of Christ

I n 1Corinthians 12:12-27 and Romans 12:4-5, the Apostle Paul gives a thesis of the similarity in composition and function of the Body of Christ to the human body. Consider the following passages from the Message (MSG) Translation:

"***The way God designed our bodies is a model for understanding our lives together as a church***: every part dependent on every other part, the parts we mention and the parts we don't, the parts we see and the parts we don't. If one part hurts, every other part is involved in the hurt, and in the healing. If one part flourishes, every other part enters into the exuberance. You are Christ's body—that's who you are! You must never forget this. Only as you accept your part of that body does your "part" mean anything". (1Cor12:25-27 MSG)

"But I also want you to think about how this keeps your significance from getting blown up into self-importance. For no matter how significant you are, it is only because of what you are a part of. An enormous eye or a gigantic hand wouldn't be a body, but a monster. What we have is one body with many parts, each its proper size and in its proper place. No part is important on its own". (1Cor12:19-20 MSG)

"In this way we are like the various parts of a human body. Each part gets its meaning from the body as a whole, not the other way around. The body we're talking about is Christ's body of chosen people. Each of us finds our meaning and function as a part of his body. But as a chopped-off finger or cut-off toe we wouldn't amount to much, would we? So since we find ourselves fashioned into all these excellently formed and marvellously functioning parts in Christ's body, let's just go ahead and be what we were made to be, ... " (Romans 12:4-5 MSG)

Also consider Eph4:16, from The Passion Translation
    "For his body has been formed in his image and is closely joined together and constantly connected as one. And every member has been given divine gifts to contribute to the growth of all; and as these gifts operate effectively throughout the whole body, we are built up and made perfect in love".

Contrary however to the ethos of these passages, the prevalent message in many churches is about self-actualization, personal ambitions, individual and independent success. With most everybody striving for autonomous glory, the intricate yet superb idea of intentional and practical community is often jarring to people's sensibilities.

On the other hand, careful consideration of the posited similarity and model shows some very important implications:

Intelligent participation - Although physical body parts don't get to choose whether or not they work in community with the body they are a part of but are directed by the brain, the Bible verses that speak about the Body of Christ teach that each member of the Body gets to make a personal choice whether to participate or not, even when clearly directed by Christ (through the scriptures and by the Holy Spirit) to do so. We choose. We decide. We each have our place yet we choose whether or not to find it. We choose whether or not to embrace it. We choose whether or not to serve the Body the way Christ intended.

Intentional Devotion - upon choosing to be part of and to participate in (a local expression of) the body, all the body parts must be devoted to the whole body, through personal, practical and enduring care (true love). This intentional devotion will require a commitment to living by, through and for the benefit of our immediate and, or, assigned communities, and ultimately the universal body.

Mutual edification - each part needs the other for growth, strength and effectiveness. Every part supplies something that builds up other parts and the whole body, and every part must work to that end. Every part is attached to another and is the conduit for information and nurture of those directly linked parts. The strength of the body depends on the mutual strengthening of the body parts.

Common purpose and goals - all the body parts are committed to achieving the same common objectives. In the same way that all of an athlete's or engineer's or musician's body parts concentrate on the achievement of any given goal, so should the parts of (and members of various hubs of) the Body of Christ.

Coordinated effort - even though they may all be trying to achieve the same objective, this is best done through a harmonized system. To avoid divergence and dissipation there is a need for coordinated convergence of efforts.

Physical proximity and connectedness - and all the above are most effectively and efficiently achieved when and because the body parts are all (physically) connected; they are all on the same property so to speak. When the people (the body parts) are connected at a 'dwelling' level, they are more efficient and productive, and able to interact in a much more blessed and rewarding way. It is time for the Body of Christ to come together, and indeed dwell together.

Psalm 133 - Behold, how good and how pleasant it is For brothers to **live together** in unity! It *[living together in unity]* is like the precious oil on the head, Running down upon the beard, As on Aaron's beard, The oil which ran down upon the edge of his robes. It *[living together in unity]* is like the dew of Hermon coming down upon the mountains of Zion; For the Lord commanded the blessing there *[where? living together in unity]* —life forever. *[emphasis mine]*

    ('live' - yāšaḇ: A verb meaning to sit, to dwell, to inhabit, to endure, to stay - Strongs 3427)

Ecclesiastes 4:9-12 - Two are better than one because they have a good return for their labour; for if either of them falls, the one will lift up his companion. But woe to the one who falls when there is not another to lift him up! Furthermore, if two lie down together they keep warm, but how can one be warm alone? And if one can overpower him who is alone, two can resist him. A cord of three strands is not quickly torn apart.

I agree with Charles Moore when he writes that "to come across a dismembered human body part, like a finger or a toe, would shock and repulse us. If we would only step back and see how fractured and dismembered our lives are, we might see why restoring our lives to wholeness, as difficult as this might be, is so desperately needed. After all, this is what Christ prayed for, and it is what our world needs. Jesus prayed that we might be a community, that his followers would possess the togetherness and love and unity that he and the Father have for each other (John 17:20–26)."[6]

---

[6] Charles E Moore - Called to Community: Plough Publishing House, 2016. pages 82-87

5

Nature of the early Church

Virtually all the apostles' letters and epistles were written to bodies of people, to churches who knew that they were the churches being addressed, with regional or geographical identities. The letters were not written to individual Christians who were then to circulate it amongst all other known Christians, they were written to churches. Of course, churches are made up of individuals but they are individuals with a cohesive organic relationship; members of a body.

Most of the "you"s in the NT are plural, addressing a group. The lessons of these letters can only be sensibly applied to people in an ongoing group relationship, about how to persevere in, strengthen and add others to that relationship. Indeed the Body of Christ is called ekklēsía (Church), 'the called out ones', referring to the organic nature of the church.

When the new testament uses the reciprocal pronoun "one another" [allelon][7], e.g. Rom10:12 / 1Cor11:33 / Gal5:13, practically none of the passages make sense unless, as Charles E Moore says, "we share life together and are committed to one another. How are we to bear another person's burden unless the burden is known and unless we are willing to actually carry it? How are we to "put up with each other" unless we relate closely enough to get on each other's nerves? How are we to forgive one another unless we are in each other's lives enough to hurt and let one another down? How can we learn to submit to one another unless we struggle with differences? In other words, if we are to connect (or reconnect) our lives with one another, it will demand much more of us than we normally give. It demands that we become a church community, not just occasionally go to church or have community with others."[8]

I have come to believe that Christianity should be, and is designed to be lived and done in and as communities: bonded groups of people, dwelling in proximity, with a localised identity. The most consistent pattern or picture of Christians in the New Testament (and early church history) is of those who lived in community: attached to, growing with, responsible for and accountable to one another. Not the virtually solitary lives many of us now live, often deceiving ourselves with 'virtual' social media communities. Not the fragmented congregational events either, where 'members' may travel from far and wide to their favourite church but have very little to nothing to do with each

---

[7] Examples of 'one another' (allelon - Strongs 240): Rom10:12. 12:16, 15:14, 16:16 / 1Cor11:33, 12:25 / Gal5:13, 6:2 / 1Thess5:11, 5:13, 5:15, / Eph4:2, 4:32, 5:21 / Col3:13 / James5:16 / 1Pet1:22, 4:9, 5:5.

[8] Charles E Moore - Called to Community: Plough Publishing House, 2016. pages 82-87

other **where they live** Monday to Sunday.[9]

The apostles addressed churches and the issues in churches. Jesus also, in the (book of) Revelation of John addressed churches and issues in/with churches.

He is the head of a body and he is coming back for a body of bodies.

The NT repeatedly refers to the church as the Body of Christ, and someday soon we shall all be together, in the same place attending to the same purposes. However, for now, our unity, which is primarily spiritual, ought to be expressing itself in the heartfelt, heart-driven desire for community; enacting and practising our destiny of heavenly community, much in the same way we desire, enact and practice a lot of other things that will only find their perfect expression and fulfilment in the coming kingdom, e.g. healing, holiness, forgiveness, justice etc.

---

[9] This is no indictment on the Body of Christ or any specific church(es). It is simply a generic statement which, in my studied opinion, reflects the general outlook of 20th/21st century 'churching'. Without a doubt, there are several very good exceptions, two of which are shared in the next chapter.

6

Some bible examples

Abraham, the father of faith, lived in and built a massive community. In Genesis chapter 14, Abraham went on a rescue mission (for Lot & family) with 318 trained men born in his house(hold). And these are only the "trained men". If you considered the untrained men, all the women and children, they'd be easily over 1000 people in the community. I am quite confident that they would have had opportunities to go and start their own nuclear families (and maybe some did) but rather chose to remain integrated with Abraham's community. Lot, Abraham's cousin did separate himself and his family from Abraham's community, perhaps with a bid for independent wealth-building or simply pursuing 'his own destiny', (or a few other reasons) as so many of us do today. Yet he not only needed rescuing from marauders, by the same Abraham he left, but we also know how his story went thereafter.[10]

---

[10] I do appreciate that other factors would have contributed to Lot's lot at Sodom, but separating himself from Abraham's community certainly only weakened his spiritual and defensive strengths, and contributed to his compromised life story.

The story of **Joseph** was a story of community. At first, he had this dream and thought it was all about him being the top dog or superstar. But after several tests and, presumably, encounters with God, he came to a realisation that he was to preserve a community for God. His purpose in life and the ultimate meaning of his dream was to preserve a people for God. And it made sense for his people to live and multiply as a community - in Goshen.

It is also worth noting here that Joseph saw no conflict of interest in holding a government position and leveraging its benefits in favour of his people (not on himself).

Gen45:7,8: "God sent me before you to preserve for you a remnant in the earth, and to keep you alive by a great deliverance. "Now, therefore, it was not you who sent me here, but God; and He has made me a father to Pharaoh and lord of all his household and ruler over all the land of Egypt."

The story of **David's** life was one of community as well. When David fled for his life, he soon became the leader of a nomadic-warrior community. Most of his greatest post-Goliath exploits were done with and through this community.

1Sam22:1,2 - So David departed from there and escaped to the cave of Adullam; and when his brothers and all his father's household heard of it, they went down there to him. Everyone who was in distress, and everyone who was in debt, and everyone who was discontented (and their families?) gathered to him; and he became captain over them. Now there were about four hundred men with him. [11]

Jesus and his closest disciples were a community; for 3 years they shared life quite intimately and shared a common purse (John12:6) and, by implication, shared resources. *(Yet the man entrusted with the responsibility of managing the disciples' money broke under it —a lesson with no little significance for our mammonistic society today)* .

The early believers too must have lived in proximity as they were "breaking bread *from house to house*, they were taking their meals together with gladness and sincerity of heart" (Acts2:46)[12]. It was in this setting that poverty was eradicated as many sold possessions to provide for their various practical needs (Acts4:34). For those who had been closest to Jesus in his life and ministry, this was a natural continuation of the lifestyle they chose when they responded to his call and followed him. Some had left their homes and given up personal ambitions to walk with him, and their needs were met from the common purse. The large numbers who were added would have also followed suit.

The early Christians did not just occasionally fellowship (verb);

---

[11] As glorious as David's story is to us, I suspect that being part of this type of community, initially populated with vagabonds and vagrants and discontented and broke people, is probably more of a nightmare than a dream for most Christians.

[12] They must have lived in very close proximity to be able to sustain this pattern. They probably lived there before their conversion, yet we must consider that it was God's Providence so as to enable the necessary integration and 'light on a hill' model.

they were a fellowship (noun). They didn't go to church; they were the church. Few of us today experience life together as the early Christians did—a common, daily, material life of unity and sharing. We rush here and there, madly trying to connect with this group or that person, but still living lives that are very much our own. We follow and text each other, but actually share very little of ourselves.[13]

---

[13] Charles E Moore - Called to Community : Plough Publishing House, 2016. pages 82-87

7

Christian Community Examples

There is a long and beautiful history of successful Christian community through the centuries. To name but a few: the first century Christians, the 13th century Ethiopian Ewostathians[14], Anabaptist movements of the sixteenth century, the early Quakers and the Labadists of the seventeenth and eighteenth centuries, the early Moravians, Mennonites, Hutterites, Amish, and in many other denominations and movements, in all parts of the world, down to our present day; a 'google' of any of these names will yield very elucidating material. Many of the older movements are still thriving and newer movements are being established and growing.

---

[14] Ewostathians, or the **House of Ewostatewos**, were the disciples of Ewostatewos (lived July 15, 1273 – September 15, 1352). He was an important religious leader of the Orthodox Tewahedo during the early period of the Solomonic dynasty of Ethiopia and a forceful advocate for the observation of the Sabbath in Christianity. They lived in community, founding monasteries, even after his death.

Examples of effective community

below are three inspiring examples of community; one historic, and the other two taken from the several intentional Christian communities that are currently functioning well, even in our modern individualistic world.

These are only brief examples, but for those who wish to look wider, a fairly up to date directory of communities can be found online (see notes).[15] Please note that intentional Christian communities vary in style, and in social and theological approaches. It is unlikely that any one person would be happy with all those listed in the directory!

1 – William Wilberforce and 'The Clapham Sect'[16]

William Wilberforce (1759-1833) is probably best known as the forefront name in the abolition of slave trade, however, he did not act alone in his abolition efforts. Begun as a simple group of friends, the Clapham Sect became one of the most influential groups of evangelicals known in Britain. Named after a village just south of Westminster, Clapham grew to be

---

[15] Explore a list of Christian communities here: https://onlinechristianlibrary. com/links-to-christian-communities

[16] References:

Victoria Marple (2000) – The Clapham Sect: an investigation into the effects of deep faith in a personal God on a change effort.

Dr Richard Gathro (2001) – William Wilberforce and His Circle of Friends – summer 2001 issue of the C.S. Lewis Institute Report.

Kanayo Nwadialor & Chinedu Emmanuel Nnatuanya (2016) – Wealth and political influence in the expansion of Christian Frontiers in Contemporary Nigeria: the 'Clapham Sect' lesson.

a home for reformers and comrades. The group was sparked by a friendship between Wilberforce, Eliot Thorton and Henry Thorton.

In 1792, in the early days of the fight against slavery, these men set up to live together in a house bought by Henry after the death of his father. Wilberforce lived with the Thorntons until Wilberforce's marriage to Barbara Spooner. He and Barbara then moved into Bloomfield, one of two houses built on the grounds. The other was leased to Charles Grant, another regular member of the Clapham group. This house eventually grew to 34 bedrooms and two new separate houses contained within the gardens (Broomfield Lodge and Grant Glenelg).

The title the "Clapham Sect" was not coined until many years after the deaths of most in the group. During their lifetimes, the group was known as "the saints," which was not usually spoken about in a favourable light.

The core of the saints included the Thortons, Zachary Macaulay and his wife Selina Miles, James Stephen, Charles Middleton, William Smith, John Shore, John Venn, Charles Grant, Edward Bickersteth and Chief Justice Mansfield. Among their guests and extended friendships were Hannah More, Dean Milner, Babington, Charles Simeon, and Gisborne.

More important than the names of this group are their respective occupations, whether in Government or otherwise. Hannah More was a writer of pamphlets and plays. The saints had several Members of Parliament of which were William Smith, Wilberforce, and James Stephen. Also useful to the influence the saints had was James Stephen's occupation as a Chancery lawyer, John Venn was a preacher and also the son of a great minister. Zachary Macaulay was Governor of Sierra Leone, and John Shore was Governor-General of India. The informal, yet well-defined organization also included three bankers, Henry Thorton, Samuel Smith and Abel Smith. Sir Charles Middleton became the First Lord Barham and was a naval officer. Charles Grant had been an East India Merchant.

It has been stated that "No Prime Minister had such a cabinet as Wilberforce could summon to his assistance."[17]

This group influenced and encouraged Wilberforce to write his seminal and hugely successful book on the essentials of the Christian faith, 'A Practical View of the Prevailing Religious System of Professed Christians in the Higher and Middle Classes in This Country Contrasted with Real Christianity', (yes, that's really the title!) which also shares the story of his personal transformation upon coming to faith.

The book was hugely successful, immediately selling over 7,500 copies in the first six months. With several editions and translations by 1826, this publication brought conviction of change to a society with a degenerating culture.

Wilberforce, and His closest friend Henry Thornton, intentionally called this group around them for support in pushing through his motion for the abolition of slavery and slave trade. They desired to apply their faith in Jesus Christ to personal, social, political, national and international matters, believing they

---

[17] Lean, Grath. God's Politician .· Colorado Springs: Helmers & Howard Publishers, Inc., 1987. Pg 104

were representatives and faithful stewards of God's kingdom.

The Clapham Sect has been credited with playing a significant part in the development of Victorian morality, through their writings, their societies, their influence in Parliament, and their example in philanthropy and moral campaigns, especially against slavery. In the words of the historian Stephen Tomkins, "The ethos of Clapham became the spirit of the age."[18]

Together, this Clapham fellowship sought to make the British Empire an instrument of social and moral welfare to all people. Throughout their time together, they remained remarkably committed to these goals.

The projects undertaken by the group were not limited to slave trade abolition or reformation of manners; they founded the colony of Sierre Leone to have an accommodation for freed slaves, they founded both the British and Foreign Bible Society and the Church Missionary Society, fought to shorten the working hours of children working in the mills, and to humanize the prison system.

The group are described by Stephen Tomkins as "a network of friends and families in England, with William Wilberforce as its centre of gravity, who were powerfully bound together by their shared moral and spiritual values, by their religious mission and social activism, by their love for each other, and by marriage".[19]

---

[18] Stephen Tomkins, (2010) The Clapham Sect: How Wilberforce's circle changed Britain. Pg248

[19] Stephen Tomkins, (2010) The Clapham Sect: How Wilberforce's circle changed Britain

A unique feature of the "Clapham Sect" was the desire to live with one another, or in very close proximity to each other. Always welcome in each other's homes, the Saints were known to be "good family people." In spite of the Clapham Sect's many crusades, life in many ways was centred around their homes, with family and friendships as priorities. This was undoubtedly one of the group's important sources of vitality.

Members of this group were lifelong friends who delighted greatly in each other's marriages and families. They valued their common purpose above individual preferences and ambitions, integrating each other's passions into the common purpose. They were thorough and professional in all of their advocacy endeavours. They worshipped together regularly and they considered their faith fundamental to all aspects of life; evangelism, social action, marriage, careers, friendships, etc, all moderated and empowered by their faith.

The historian, Sir Reginald Coupland, writing on the communal strength of the Clapham Sect, described the group as a remarkable fraternity: remarkable above all else, perhaps, in its closeness, its affinity; living mostly in one little village and sharing one character, one mind, one way of life. They all devoted their lives to the service of others.

They were indeed what Wilberforce meant by 'true Christians'.

2 - The Bruderhof

The Bruderhof (/ˈbruːdərˌhɔːf/; 'place of brothers')[20] is an Anabaptist Christian movement that was founded in Germany in 1920 by Eberhard Arnold. The movement has 23 communities with a total membership of over 2700, in the United States, the United Kingdom, Germany, Austria, Paraguay, and Australia (2021 data)

Background: Born into a long line of German academics and himself a doctor of philosophy, Eberhard Arnold abandoned middle-class life to found the community now known as The Bruderhof. His own words describe his journey best: "In my youth, I tried to lead people to Jesus through the Bible, and through addresses and discussions. But there came a time when I recognized that this was no longer enough. I began to see the tremendous power of greed, of discord, of hatred, and of the sword: the hard boot of the oppressor upon the neck of the oppressed. . . . I had preached the gospel but felt I needed to do more: that the demands of Jesus were practical, and not limited to a concern for the soul. . . . I could not endure the life I was living any longer. "

His spiritual awakening had begun years earlier when, as a teenager on summer vacation at the home of 'Uncle' Ernst, his mother's cousin, he had read the New Testament with fresh eyes. Ernst, a Lutheran pastor who had lost his church position after siding with the poor weavers of the region during

---

[20] All factual information about the Bruderhof is taken from their website www.bruderhof.com, except for the business financial figures taken from 'Dun & Bradstreet' searches.

a labour dispute, impressed him deeply. By the time he returned home, Eberhard was burdened with a new consciousness of his privileges and the plight of the impoverished.

The end of the first world war in 1918 heralded little in the way of peace: there were strikes, assassinations, revolutions, and counter-revolutions, and finally the birth of the Weimar Republic. In Eberhard's words, the hour demanded a discipleship that "transcended merely edifying experiences". Increasingly he pondered the evils of mammon, the god of money and material wealth. "Most Christians have completely failed in the social sphere and have not acted as brothers to their fellow man. They have risen up as defenders of money and capitalism", he said. An alternative emerged, simple but all-consuming:

Jesus says, "Do not gather riches for yourself." That is why the members of the first church in Jerusalem distributed all they had. Love impelled them to lay everything at the apostles' feet, and the apostles distributed these goods to the poor in the church.

As he said at a lecture in 1929: "People tear themselves away from home, parents, and career for the sake of marriage; they risk their lives for the sake of wife and child. In the same vein, people must be found who are ready to sacrifice everything for the sake of this way, for the service of all people.

Community is alive wherever these small bands of people meet, ready to work for the one great goal, to belong to the one true future. Already now we can live in the power of this future; already now we can shape our lives in accordance with God and his kingdom. This kingdom of love, free of mammon, is drawing near. Change your thinking radically so that you will be ready for the coming order!"

Jürgen Moltmann, a German theologian, wrote that Aberhard's voice is "authentically prophetic and as immediately compelling...... it is the voice of a Christian just as radical as Christoph Blumhardt before him and Dietrich Bonhoeffer after him. It is a wake-up call for the religiously sedated and socially domesticated Christendom of the Western world. I read and hear it as "the voice of one crying in the wilderness". [21]

"It may seem strange that such an insignificant group could experience such lofty feelings of peace and community, but it was so", Eberhard wrote shortly before his death. "It was a gift from God. And only one antipathy was bound up in our love – a rejection of the systems of civilization; a hatred of the falsities of social stratification; an antagonism to the spirit of impurity; an opposition to the moral coercion of the clergy. The fight that we took up was a fight against these alien spirits. It was a fight for the spirit of God and Jesus Christ."

Membership: The Bruderhof believes in and practises community of goods and a common purse. Once someone has become a member, all of his or her earnings and inheritances are given to the church community, and each receives necessities such as food, clothing, and housing, *never to be in need again*. Also, no Bruderhof unit/community is to be richer or poorer than another.

---

[21] Jürgen Moltmann. *Eberhard Arnold's Unsettling Message*. Plough Publishing. June 2014.

Business: The Bruderhof run a variety of businesses that provide income to run their communities and provide common work for the members who almost all work onsite, although offsite work is not forbidden and is not unusual.

Community Playthings was developed during the 1950s and soon became the Bruderhof's main source of income. Community Playthings designs and manufactures quality wooden classroom and play environments and toys for schools and daycare centres. The business is run by the communities in the United States and the United Kingdom. ($22.7m turnover - 2019 Dun & Bradstreet)

Rifton Equipment, run by some of the American communities, designs, manufactures and sells mobility and rehabilitation equipment for disabled adults and children. It was founded in 1977. ($100.5m turnover - 2019: Dun & Bradstreet)

Danthonia Designs is the business that supports the Australian Bruderhofs. It specializes in hand-carved three-dimensional signage and was founded in 2001. ($5.1m turnover - 2019: Dun & Bradstreet)

Outreach: "As often as possible, the Bruderhof church community sends out brothers and sisters to proclaim the gospel. In doing so, our prayer is that the original apostolic commission might become a reality today as it was in New Testament times: for Christ's messengers to be equipped with the full authority of the Spirit, going into all the world to invite people to the great feast of the kingdom of God. We pray that God grants this gift somewhere, whether to us or to others. But whatever the measure of grace he gives us, he sends us out as envoys of his kingdom, and we desire to obey."

1. The Bruderhof is actively involved in the neighbourhoods that surround its communities and in the world at large. The Bruderhof sees justice and the works of mercy as a gospel command. They foster many ecumenical relationships with other churches and denominations. For instance, in 2019 the Bruderhof collaborated with the Coptic church to commemorate the Coptic martyrs killed by ISIS. Members met the Pope in Rome in 2004. They also collaborate with several parachurch organisations especially in the area of relief.

2. Bruderhof members serve on school boards, volunteer at soup kitchens, prisons and hospitals, and work with local social service agencies such as the police to provide food and shelter for those in need of help. They are active supporters of various international aid organizations, such as Oxfam, Save the Children, Tear Fund, and World Vision.

3. The Bruderhof's Plough Publishing House publishes books and a magazine called Plough Quarterly. Plough publishes spiritual classics, inspirational books, and children's books, some of which are available as free downloads. Some of the books are written by Bruderhof members, but others are not.

4. In response to the Columbine High School massacre in 1999, the Bruderhof and Detective Steven McDonald created a program of school assemblies that have now reached tens of thousands of youths in the United States and the United Kingdom. Operating under the name "Breaking the Cycle", speakers with forgiveness stories speak to children at school assemblies.

5. The Bruderhof's 'Acts 2 Campus Network' is a campus ministry committed to following Jesus together by finding

practical ways to love each other and our neighbours. God wants to transform our world, here and now, and we're finding that when you truly love your neighbour as yourself, peace and justice become a reality

Conclusion: I have read several writings of Aberhard Arnold, *(which I've found incredibly insightful, deeply spiritual and very practical),* many other Plough publications, and the Bruderhof's very detailed statements of faith and operations. Based on what I do know from these and other non-Bruderhof material, I find the movement very admirable and inspiring. They have tweaked, adapted and refined over the years to better live out their foundational ethos in an ever-changing world. Now over 100 years old, they are still growing from strength to strength.

3 – New Covenant Community, Greenwich NY

I invited my good friend Pastor Thomas Bowden, founding leader of New Covenant Community (upstate NY), to contribute to this discourse on community. Below is his response which I am grateful for as it adds great value to the understanding of the subject.

"As I write about my understanding of community, I am careful not to present it in an idyllic way. Community crosses the line between church life and domestic life which manifests dimensions of human nature and character that most churches choose not to deal with. The blessings of community are not only because of what we have but because of what we are willing to get rid of.

When I came to the Lord in 1970, I was soon disappointed in the independence of the people in the church and the lack of loyalty toward each other. Even Spirit-filled church services go only so far in building relationships between God's people. It is easy to love each other in a Spirit-filled meeting, but that love gets tested when the same people work together, eat together, or labour together in the Spirit and in the natural toward the common good. A group of people going to church does not create 'a people'. A congregation of 'I' people does not create a 'we' people. Community challenges more areas of our fallen nature than traditional church structure and is therefore more effective in preparing God's people to stand in the end days.

Christian communities vary. Each one seeks a measure of separation from the unhealthy overdependence on the systems of the world that are under the sway of the wicked one. The degree of separation and the means of separation define each community. The most well-known communities, such as the Shakers, Amish, and Mennonites follow the Anabaptist traditions. The Shakers, for example, were communal with all members sharing a common purse. Others simply share a common vision of oneness in God. Each structure has its unique blessings and problems. Most communities see secular government as man's alternative to the rule of God, having an appreciation for its role in maintaining law and order but have limited confidence in their relationships with the church.

We do not believe in a survivalist mentality; this is neither the gospel nor what the church was called to. Our relationship to natural things is to be good stewards and be responsible people. We also know there will be less and less room for God's people in secular society as the day of the Lord approaches. Those who believe they have separated themselves completely from this world are not being honest with themselves. This may have been possible in times of agrarian cultures of the past but not today.

We do not believe we can fulfil God's purposes on the earth when all our resources are committed to daily natural survival. Our position on natural skills is a simple one: It is good for us to know how to do these things. For example – the cost of lumber has reached an unprecedented high. It is good for us to know how to clear land, cut down trees, mill our own wood, and build with our own hands. Part of our vision is to free ourselves and each other from as much debt to this world as possible. We are not in a delusion of our need for such things as gas, machinery, tires and so much more that the world may provide, we simply want to do for ourselves as much as we reasonably can. There is an unhealthy pride (and weakness) that comes with the belief that one has delivered himself from any dependency on the world. Even separationist groups such as the Amish are dependent on customers from the world to buy their goods.

We believe if we raise our children to be spiritually strong and naturally capable, we will have done the will of God to prepare them for whatever comes. We believe hard times are coming and that the Lord is giving us reasonable, rational, sensible, and spiritual direction in preparation for those times.

Sometimes I think about the Lord's promise of an end day outpouring of His Spirit. The vision of end-day revival presented by most Church denominations is one of the earth being filled with churches of their denomination; bigger and better churches with more pews and better sound systems. Denominations will be in competition for the souls of men who remain entrenched, dependent upon, and in debt to the world. There will hardly be deliverance from the spider's web but simply a robust development of its religious arm. I do not believe this wisdom is from above. I believe an outpouring of God's Spirit is going to result in swarms of people craving communion with God's people in settings that facilitate spiritual and natural life together. This is most viably achieved through and in community."

When did you start an intentional community?

The church started in 1975 and I was following the traditional liturgy of the Pentecostal Church but felt we were on the wrong track and were frustrating the Holy Ghost. Souls were coming to the Lord, but I was conflicted with what they were being brought to. In 1976 I began introducing the importance of closer fellowship. We began sharing meals and meeting in homes as well as in the church building. The surrounding pentecostal churches were uncomfortable with this, and with good reason; people meeting outside of church services tended to lead to schisms. We chose to continue on our course and deal with schisms, and those who caused them, as we went along. People began moving, to live closer to the church so we could share as much of our lives together as possible. We began to cross-pollinate each other with natural and spiritual resources such as skills and talents.

We are based in the countryside but if we lived in the city, we would have purchased an apartment building, renovated the first floor for worship services, lived in the apartments, eaten together often, and encouraged cottage industry.

Top main reasons for going this route

The lack of "true to life" lifestyle of traditional church structure. Pursuing community meant our church program became the building of our spiritual and domestic lives together. Most lost souls are not looking for a church but spiritual truth and life in the real world.

My burden for community began before I understood what it was the Lord was putting in my heart. While pastoring in a pentecostal church in the early 1970s, I found a recurring pattern happening each week. Our Sunday services were blessed, and the Spirit of the Lord was at work in the hearts of the people. Men of God ministered in the Spirit during church services, and the Spirit did His work, only to see that work frustrated by the framework of church structure and the culture we were living in. Church became an instrument of preservation and maintenance, not growth and maturity.

But Mondays were a day of much counselling. Most of this counselling was more about domestic family matters than spiritual matters. The issues usually involved husbands who were not as involved with their families as they should be because they were always working to support an over-extended lifestyle; many mothers also worked for the same reasons. Children were not being raised according to the biblical model and this also created problems. In most of these situations, I found the cause for deterioration in these families to be the draining of three basic resources from the home: time, energy, and money; emphasizing one was always at the expense of the other two. It was becoming apparent to me that the church was following the same secular models for success, with underlying motives of status over stature and symbolism over substance.

Creating an image is not the same as being a testimony.

Having many meetings with many guest speakers built people up spiritually but also seemed to be exacerbating the problem of limited resources. This was troubling to me in light of the scriptures that admonish us to gather together more often as we see "the day" approaching (Heb10:25). Clearly, a simpler lifestyle would be an enormous help. A cultural change whereby our domestic lives and spiritual lives were not in competition but complemented each other was the answer. Reconciling natural work with spiritual worship and communion facilitated both needs.

In short, community is simply the marriage of practicality and spirituality in a structure that re-channels our natural resources of time, energy, and money in a more fruitful manner, and our spiritual resources into the framework of a more pliable wineskin.

Mission and vision

Our mission and vision are to live out a testimony of a powerfully supernatural God who is also sane, orderly, and practical. Jesus is the perfect reconciliation of the natural and spiritual world without being carnal or spiritually strange. We also emphasize growing in understanding, embracing sound doctrine, and strengthening the family, the home, and our relationships with each other.

Leadership model

We recognize and acknowledge any gifts and callings within our fellowship, but I am reluctant to assign titles. In our early

years, I was in fellowship with independent, charismatic minis-
ters who insisted on almost everyone having titles. I believe this
has its biblical place but found myself being pressured to show
legitimacy with an array of elders, deacons, prophets, teachers,
etc. For us, this proved to be a mistake. Titles can change some
people. Presently, we are doing well with some elders and a
pastor. No one's gift is being restrained for lack of title. I do see
ordinations in our near future.

Our fellowship respects men of God but most of them have
passed away. We find the writings of men from one and two
hundred years ago to be closer to the heart and mind of God than
what is generally marketed today.

Membership

Membership begins with the first act of salvation which is
Acts 2:38. From here a person must bring forth fruit worthy of
repentance. A person can pass through Acts 2:38 yet remain
a perpetual visitor by not growing in God nor refining their
relationship with the Lord or His people. I am thankful whenever
someone passes through the outer gate but saddened when they
live in the outer court and do not dwell in the secret place of the
Most High. As long as they do not create trouble or confusion,
they may remain in that court although the Lord continually
beckons them to come into His holy place.

Family autonomy

We respect family autonomy and are careful not to trespass
against it. We also believe the autonomous family has a responsibility to the corporate body. The life in the home and in the
body must be compatible. As the church does not trespass on
the home, so the home cannot trespass against the church.

Absolute musts and must-nots

This could easily become a long list with most items agreeable to most Christians. I will abbreviate it as much as possible.

Must:

- be born again according to Acts 2:38
- obey the moral commandments
- believe the Bible is the written Word of God and that the Bible is the final word of authority in our lives
- support the church community
- take responsibility for one's family
- be in agreement with the doctrines of the church
- submit to church authority and be willing to take correction
- put the peace of the church and the unity of the saints above personal desires or opinions
- think in plurality.

Must not:

- cause confusion or division in the church
- undermine the ministry or the brethren
- bring the world's value systems into the church
- be selfish, self-centred, self-seeking or self-promoting.

Electives:

There is Biblical precedent for people honouring God with covenants that are in harmony with the law but not commanded by the law. We have agreed together to commit ourselves to codes of dress that honour God and are according to His Word. This is done for the sake of others. Those who are truly searching for truth have an innate sense that truth will look different, sound different, live different, and dress differently than the world around them. When such a person comes to the Lord, they are more than willing to do or be anything that would please the Lord.

We believe the world is rapidly deteriorating into all sorts of perversions. Because the distinctions between man and woman are being perverted, we have chosen to follow the biblical guidelines for the sexes even though such things may be considered archaic by modern society. This obedience is not for our salvation but a message of hope for those looking for clarity, order, and sanity in a world of confusion and perversion, which are being sold as progression. The message we are sending is that we do not agree with nor belong to the value systems of this world. We have agreed to stand together in this commitment. What one man mocks will give another man hope.

Membership numbers

When we began in 1975 the number of adults was about ten.

Currently (April 2021) there are slightly more than 200 people including children.

Since our beginning, hundreds of people have passed through our doors. Most of those were looking for something other than who we were or what we believed yet they wanted the fruit. In short, they wanted to be grafted into a fruitful vine but not produce fruit themselves; some even despised the root. In our formative years, we were willing, as we are today, to make whatever changes necessary to grow and mature in the Lord. Some earlier changes were mistakes as we realized we were not advancing the Kingdom but compromising it. Compromises brought influxes of people, and correcting the compromises drove them away. We passed through the erroneous belief that people in the building were people in the church and people in the church were people in the Lord. This gave the impression of a growing church but was simply a growing number of occupants. The true church was suffering under the adulterous mix of other gospels, other righteousnesses, other visions, and other motives for being there. We suffered repeated doses of the spirit of antichrist from within the church and have become familiar with its nature and modes of operation. Most of the attempts to destroy this church have come through professing Christians who mistakenly view Christianity from a perspective of self-gain and not self-sacrifice. This should not be a surprise since the antichrist's ultimate goal is to sit in the temple of God and defile it with his piggish nature. We are familiar with the Lord's shaking of His Church and are thankful for it. We are thankful for what gets shaken off and increasingly thankful for what remains.

Age demography

Our ages range from newborn to 83 years. We have not experienced generation gaps as our lives continue to be woven together. The children love and respect the adults and the adults love the children.

Range of (non-community) vocations and careers

The range of vocations and careers include medical, financial, legal, and educational professionals; engineers; construction trades; military; law enforcement; salesmen; craftsmen; as well as others. While a number of our young men and women are in college (the way we relate to college is a topic of its own), our present retirement population is steadily growing.

Size of community land

The original parcel, purchased in 1979, was about 150 acres. About 45 acres were eventually surveyed; they are now privately owned. The remaining land (1979 purchase) plus 70 newly acquired acres is community property. The community also owns four buildings on the main street in the neighbouring village.

Number of homes and ownership model of homes/land

Fourteen family homes onsite, with ten more families owning homes in the neighbourhood. The property lots (home and land) are privately owned and sizes range from two and a half acres to five acres. Some homes have rental apartments for people in the church.

Our original vision was to free up and facilitate those who had a heart and burden to build the kingdom. Poor vetting and anxiousness to progress resulted in some bad decisions. The Lord has been faithful, and will continue to be, to correct our mistakes and redeem the land to its original purposes. Our plan was for homes to be no larger or more complicated than necessary to raise a family. In some instances, this too went awry. The land itself is gravel which is good for building but not the best for agriculture. We do encourage some level of homesteading for practical use of the land and teaching practical skills to the children.

Community projects, ventures and businesses

Besides carrying out lots of property maintenance for members, we are currently working on several Windy Hill Road projects: converting a large garage into a fibre arts studio; building a post and beam pavilion, as well as building several other out-buildings. In the village centre, we own 2 reasonably large properties 'rescued' from demolition several years back. They house our offices and some of our community education & training projects. We are renovating a basement into a pottery studio and converting one of the other buildings into a craft shop. At present, the craft shop (opening later this year) and the Mosaic Workshop will be our only (income) businesses in the village.

Ownership model of joint property and businesses

The joint property is in the church's name and is available for use to those within the church. Recently, we parcelled off acreage for our cemetery.

When we were operating the village breakfast cafe some people worked on salary while others volunteered their time for cleaning and food prep. Our craft shop will have a salaried overseer and shop items will be sold on commission. We will insist that the goods to be sold will also be works of excellent craftsmanship. As our breakfast cafe was our testimony to the public so will our craft shop also be. The purpose for the store is not just to provide an outlet for people to sell their products, but it must represent the excellence and order of our God in His church.

Gospel outreach

Having come out of a church structure that had intense outreach programs, I found them to be the expensive, time-consuming, and mechanizing of something that should come naturally. People who love what they have should not need to be trained in how to sell it. Most evangelistic programs are designed to get people to attend meetings. My experience has been that most people who need the Lord are not looking for another church to go to. Most of the people who come are church people looking for something new and exciting to tickle their ears. They then decide to join the church which is often the beginning of problems for everybody. We are here and quite visible for anyone seeking the reality of God. Those who hunger for righteousness will respond to the verbal and obvious testimony of those not selling a product or meeting a quota. If it is not in someone's heart to tell others of the good thing they have found, then we would rather they not pretend. In our culture, people have grown weary of all the sales pitches. They desire help and will readily respond to those who are sincerely willing to provide the help they need. Our people are not silent about the Lord and we pretty much live in a fishbowl. Our church program is our daily life and how we live it is.

Relationship with the local region

Our relationships in the local region have been interesting. It is no secret that we are here, and there have been diverse interpretations of us through the years. Rumour certainly travels faster than truth. When we first came to the area, there was a lot of suspicion regarding us. This is to be expected, and we never faulted people for being apprehensive about us. We understood that time would reveal that we are not a threat. The work we have done on the land and on the buildings in the village have earned the respect of many people. The years that we had the café worked wonders for our reputation. As people have come to respect the Amish for their diligence, honesty and work ethic, so have these become part of our testimony. The integrity of our business dealings has gained respect from the businesses in the area. I am confident that our relationships in the area are particularly good and those who seek to discredit us have little traction.

Any other relevant information

Our vision through the years has not changed but it has developed and matured in stages. Although we have always had a strong emphasis on teaching it now occupies the bulk of our vision. We believe we are advancing the Kingdom of God by increasing the worth of those in it: worth to God, self, family, community, and even to the world. This is our generational vision that each generation would inherit the scriptural promises of gold, silver, precious stones, and the godly adornments that the Lord has promised to His Church.

We believe that the godly character and the good work of each generation would increasingly gain the blessings of God as well as the respect of men. When persecution arises, it will be more difficult to accuse such a people as this; it will be easier to fault those who simply go to church.

8

The Dream (& issues)

I dream of communities of visionary members who all identify with a common and singular passion of demonstrating
'a city of light set on a hill, where our heartfelt desire is
for His name and for the fame of Him, and speaking the truth
in love, we grow up in all aspects into Christ, being fitted and
held together by what every person supplies, according to the
efficient devotion of each individual, causing the growth of the
body in love'. [Mat5:13 / Isa26:8 / Eph4:15-16]

Bruce Waltke, the renowned Bible-Hebrew scholar, coined the
proverb that the "The Righteous", in the book of Proverbs, "are
willing to disadvantage themselves to advantage the community."[22] They are therefore those who value the bottom line
of community benefit, in both their production and personal
profit.

---

[22] Westminster Theological Journal (WTJ) 70 (2008)
      (Bruce K. Waltke is Professor of Old Testament at Reformed Seminary,
   Orlando, Fla)

What it would look like – Goshen Again

Biblical Goshen was initially populated by one extended family: Jacob (Israel) and his sons and their families. As the family grew and extended, they all still chose to live in the same region, rather than disperse. Although they would have had some need to trade with the wider area, the Egyptians, they would *(most probably, even as many Jewish communities still do today)* have primarily and mostly traded amongst themselves within their own cultural and religious value system. This of course would have boosted the total wealth of Goshen and of the individual citizens.

In time, they grew into that great nation that became a threat in Pharaoh's mind. As we know, even though for a season they experienced great injustice from their world, Goshen prospered and was not touched by any of the plagues, but rather ended up acquiring enough wealth to kick-start a nation.

That Israel lived together geographically, whilst in Egypt, is made clear in Exodus 8:22 where God said "But on that day I will set apart **the land of Goshen, where My people are living,** so that no swarms of flies will be there, in order that you may know that I, the LORD, am in the midst of the land. " And "**only in the land of Goshen, where the sons of Israel were,** there was no hail."*(Exodus 9:26)*

Goshen starts small and grows big, by the promise and presence of God. And Goshen thrives on and is kept by the power of God.

My friend, Carlton B. Williams – Lead Pastor, Highlife Church, Lagos, argues that "The proof of the presence of God in the midst of people is not our theology. It is the fact that no matter what happens in Egypt, there is a Goshen." Therefore even as biblical Egypt represents the world, Goshen would represent the church; we might live in the world but live as Goshen in the world - together.

Goshen-again will be groups of people intentionally living in very close proximity, ideally as immediate neighbours on the same land, considered as a collective alliance; sharing common beliefs, purpose, interests, social values and projects, and practising common ownership and responsibility. The group defines and agrees on the level of commonality in all areas especially regarding individual and family autonomy.

Some common reactions

By and large, I believe that too many Christians have been brought up to simply live wherever they like; mostly convenient for work, and they would commute to church meetings. Few have probably ever heard a positive message about or seen or experienced a good example of community. It is therefore quite understandable that there would be misgivings about and resistance to this not-so-novel biblical truth.

Considering the self-investment and solidarity that an intentional Goshen type community requires, and how so many of us are quite tethered to the world system and enmeshed in the fashions/philosophies of the age, it will take serious revelation and deliverance to un-yoke us from the mill that promises independent success and personal glory.

Christians are strongly commanded to "not be conformed to this world (this age), [fashioned after and adapted to its external, superficial customs], but be transformed (changed) by the [entire] renewal of your mind [by its new ideals and its new attitude], so that you may prove [for yourselves] what is the good and acceptable and perfect will of God, even the thing which is good and acceptable and perfect [in His sight for you]." (Rom12 :2 AMP)

Yet we tend to uncritically follow the same 'normal' or 'cookie cutter' systems of living as defined by our local, popular or ethnic culture, and look with suspicion upon those who deviate from that norm.

Ideas of intentional community would generally receive one of the following types of responses. Each response contains just enough valid truth or concern to strengthen inertia.

Spiritual response: such as... 'the Lord is with us everywhere', 'we are already the spiritual Goshen wherever we may be', etc.

These are all technically correct, however as 'spiritual' as they may sound, the responses mostly lack practical investment or effective changes to the status quo, especially such that benefit or strengthen an intermingling collective. Any application of such ideas, if at all even possibly applicable, is entirely individually autonomous, and any (claimed) results are difficult to appraise and usually of very little gospel and kingdom impact.

Light of the world response: the argument usually is that we have to live scattered around the ungodly in order to 'reach' them for Christ.

We do indeed have to mix with non-Christians to reach them

for Christ but we do not necessarily have to live with them. If we are honest with ourselves, hardly anyone has 'evangelism' as a motivation for their choice of house or neighbourhood, rather, it's usually status or investment yield, or commuting convenience (to work especially) or simply very personal preference.

I would suggest that this 'light of the world' response is a cover for the lack of true mutual accountability. We love from a distance, quite literally. We actually just want to be able to do what we want to do, how we choose, when we choose, without too much 'interference' from other believers, so we mostly distance ourselves. I suspect that very few Christians actually preach the gospel to our immediate neighbours anyways. Yes, when did you last, if ever, preach to your residential neighbours? We keep living virtually solitary lives, deceiving ourselves with 'virtual' social media communities and confusing congregation with belonging.

[exception: if God particularly sends a person(s) to serve a particular purpose somewhere; this would be missionary in nature, and could be solitary].

Briefly considered, the biblical light of the world is (should be) an illuminating and clarifying influence on, and a visible and viable example of 'thine kingdom come, thine will be done on earth' to the peoples and systems of the world; and the salt of the earth is meant to be a purifying and preserving influence on the earth, and this is best done by purposefully engaging the fractured and broken issues of the land/issues.

Spirit-filled and well structured community will achieve both principles, certainly a lot more effectively than solitary individuals or families living most of their lives in the miasma of unsupportive residential areas.

Fear of loss: people are generally afraid of losing out especially in the financial or material equations. After all, if my possessions or excesses are constantly servicing others' very visible needs, how will I be able to fully satisfy my own pleasures and indulgences?

There is most often the irrational fear that everyone else will not be pulling their weight and I will be the one losing out! How will I ever build my own kingdom: praising myself and receiving praise? Perhaps we forget that "the person who loves his life and pampers himself will miss true life! But the one who detaches his life from this world and abandons himself to me, will find true life and enjoy it forever" (Jn12:25)

The love of the brethren in community is very personal, practical and enduring, yet the community must challenge members with responsibility for the consequences of their actions; we must attach the same priority for spiritual things as well as for day to day social issues. Character and integrity should be major parts of our faith, not just the ability to quote scripture, speak in tongues and attend meetings.

"Community that is Christocentric demonstrates love's victory over death, lived by ordinary people, in union with Christ, by the grace of his victory." (Basil Pennington - Christian author)

Knee-jerk reaction of comparing any idea of community with the bad examples of failed and unhealthy communities.

This is both an accusation of the devil and our human tendency to exaggerate the few bad examples whilst minimising the several good examples of very successful, healthy, thriving, stable and enduring communities. Besides, just because many marriages and families fail does not make marriage and family bad or dangerous. Same with any constituted group e.g.

companies, nations, NGOs, etc. Because some of them are corrupt or because some fail does not negate their necessity or effectiveness, just as much as the apparent success of any system does not prove its goodness or godliness.

I believe that at the bottom of this is a fear of death (*of self*) really, yet "a single grain of wheat will never be more than a single grain of wheat unless it drops into the ground and dies. Because then it sprouts and produces a great harvest of wheat… .." (Jn12:24 TPT)

Fear of unresolvable schisms arising from differences in culture, religious/theological background, personalities, vision and ambitions, desires, etc.

Constant proximity will inevitably lead to varying degrees of disagreements and problems, from which community members can not simply 'walk away' or 'go home', as we mostly do with 'normal' church; even in churches with good networks. This consideration understandably creates a feeling of anxiety and aversion in many. However, this would be exactly the type of consideration that Christians are exhorted to resolve "by being of the same mind, maintaining the same love, united in spirit, intent on one purpose. Do nothing from selfishness or empty conceit, but with humility consider one another as more important than yourselves; do not merely look out for your own personal interests, but also for the interests of others. Have this attitude in yourselves which was also in Christ Jesus." (Phil2:2-5) This is most effectively achieved in community. [23]

---

[23] Please refer to 'Nature of early church' chapter for a more in-depth understanding.

"We must live in community because we are compelled by the same Spirit that has led to community time and again since the days of biblical prophecy and early Christianity. We must live in community because God wants us to respond to the unclear longings of our time with a clear answer of faith." (Eberhard Arnold – Founder of The Bruderhof Community, 1920)[24]

---

[24] Why we live in community. Eberhard Arnold. Plough Publishing. 1995.

9

Hallmarks of Goshen-again

The presence of the Spirit of God will be our source, inspiration, power and direction. We truly need a fresh infilling of the Spirit to embark on this incredible journey. Only those inspired by and empowered by this infilling will be able to courageously connect with other like-minded people to do this.

The community (groups) will welcome anyone that loves the Father, Son and Spirit. Everything else is graced. This type of community will attract searchers and committed alike, members in different developmental stages. The goal is that with such a loving, vibrant and Spirit-centred presence, we grow into that stature of the harmonious, efficient, productive and joyful body.

Goshen-again would be a true light of the world by exemplifying what a truly good and godly community or *integrated neighbourhood* looks like. Jesus gave us "a new commandment: Love each other just as much as I have loved you. For when you demonstrate the same love I have for you by loving one another, *everyone will know* that you're my true followers" (John 13:34-35 TPT), and John reinforces it by saying "we know that we have passed out of death into life, because we love the brethren" (1Jn 3:14). Love is that litmus test and evidencing of our spiritual transformation and true discipleship. This is not just denominational affiliation, congregational affection or even doctrinal agreement. This love is personal, practical, enduring, often sacrificial, constantly intermingling, and commonly purposeful. How is this possible and sustainable except in integrated community hubs/groups? Or at least concentrated in chosen residential estates.

Goshen-again groups would enact the redemption from the Adamic curse and all of its ramifications, even as the Holy Spirit injects joy into the community because of their unity. How good and delightful it is for brethren to live together in unity (psalm 133:1). This picture of 'delightful living together' is of physical geographic connectedness, sharing the same space on an ongoing basis, more than simply being able to get along without actually sharing a life together.

In Goshen, we can best be our brothers' and sisters' keepers if they are also our physical neighbours. Our relationships will be enriched, our ungodliness challenged, our marriages fortified and peer-supported, our children nurtured and pro-tected together, our mental health and emotional wellbeing strengthened, spirituality deepened, poverty eradicated, and our reality clarified, together as a people. Nobody will ever really be alone or lack in such self-sustaining communities.

Goshen dwellers would share some common goals and aspirations which they would work at realising, and personal aspirations will always benefit and be supported by the community too, in the spirit of true unity and agreement.

Goshen would constantly flow in the spirit of wisdom and revelation and excellence. Goshen would practice and innovate in various areas of science, technology, agriculture, literature, arts, education, etc. We would both sell and invest to/in the world. Goshen would add diversity and value to its wider geographical regions.

Goshen does not mean we can't be gainfully employed in 'the outside world', just that we live in deliberate spiritual communities that shape our lifestyles and wellbeing; by the supply of every person. Members would of course be of various trades and professional disciplines and can be employed wherever they can, without restrictions.

In Goshen, poverty and lack will be eradicated from the communities. Distrust and fear of loss will be overcome and banished by the lively and very transformative power of love. Sickness and disease will be hardly known; as the community is strengthened, defended and healed by the power of God. All this according to the pattern of the early church animated and empowered by the Holy Spirit.

Acts2:44, 45: And all those who had believed were together and had all things in common; and they began selling their property and possessions and were sharing them with all, as anyone might have need.

Acts4:32-35: And the congregation of those who believed were of one heart and soul; and not one of them claimed that anything belonging to him was his own, but all things were common property to them. And with great power the apostles were giving testimony to the resurrection of the Lord Jesus, and abundant grace was upon them all. For there was not a needy person among them, for all who were owners of land or houses would sell them and bring the proceeds of the sales and lay them at the apostles' feet, and they would be distributed to each as any had need.

10

Shaping the dream

I dream of a community of visionary members who all identify with a common and singular passion of demonstrating 'a city set on a hill where our heartfelt desire is for His name and for the fame of Him, and speaking the truth in love, we grow up in all aspects into Christ, being fitted and held together by what every person supplies, according to the efficient devotion of each individual, causing the growth of the body in love'. [Mat5:13 / Isa26:8 / Ep 4:15-16]

"Community is an educational fellowship of mutual help and correction, of shared resources, and of work, a true community is a covenant made in free-willing surrender and sacrifice. As such it fights for the existence of the church. "[25] It is "simply the marriage of practicality and spirituality in a structure that re-channels our natural resources of time, energy, and money in a more fruitful manner, and our spiritual resources into

---

[25] Eberhard Arnold

the framework of a more pliable wineskin"[26], and a "self-sustaining ecosystem that generates all it needs to thrive. It is a gift that keeps giving"[27].

It is my hope that many people will catch the vision and want to walk or run with it, based on an understanding of and commitment to the ideal - inspired and empowered by the Holy Spirit.

The modalities and logistics of an intentional Christian community will have to be sensitively drawn up in a simple memorandum of understanding (MOU), in the clearest language possible. Below are some considerations.

Personal accountability - each member is personally accountable ultimately to God, for knowing and keeping His word & will, and may not be dominated or manipulated into relinquishing that responsibility or violating their conscience. There must however be a level of mutual accountability and peer appraisal in the spirit of fostering "being of the same mind, maintaining the same love, united in spirit, intent on one purpose". (Phil 2:2). There should be an organically developed understanding of community beliefs and expectations; these should remain organic and reasonably flexible, however, the community must challenge members with responsibility for the consequences of their actions; we must attach the same priority for spiritual things as well as for day to day social issues.

---

[26] Tom Bowden

[27] Dr. Akindotun Merino

Vocation - members should be free to pursue any vocation or career, however, as Christians, our vocations should somehow serve the Body of Christ and the kingdom of God. If we are driven by the purpose of building the body and 'thy kingdom come', then our vocations will contribute to both by also employing our skills, faculties, experience, influence, products, income and wealth to build and nurture the Body of Christ in every possible way. The church as a body and organisation has several needs – spiritual, material, logistical, etc – that are met as each member fully invests themselves in the cause of Christ and his kingdom. Romans 12:1 [AMP] appeals to us "to make a decisive dedication of your bodies *[presenting all your members and faculties]* as a living sacrifice, holy (devoted, consecrated) and well pleasing to God, which is your reasonable *(rational, intelligent)* service and spiritual worship". *(emphasis mine)*

Joint industry & enterprise - devise projects that demand integration and collaboration, for example, farming and food production, manufacturing, education, technology, services, local and wider region & national politics, etc., all to deepen communion, strengthen community values, building region-al/national profile of the community, generating wealth for kingdom purpose and posterity, contributing to nation-building through political participation.

Eradication of poverty - The community should jointly de-termine a poverty threshold and ensure that no one in the community lives below that line. Eradication of poverty through benevolent contributions, personal development and market-place empowerment.

Family sovereignty - although the community is of like-minded believers who are striving for deeper communion and further integration, each family unit will remain sovereign. The children will be directly subject to their own parents, and wives directly submitted to their own husbands. Husbands are directly responsible for their wives and children. Families should maintain their own personalities and preferences in personal matters, to the extent that such sovereignty does not disrupt or fracture the general harmony and integrity of the community. For instance, home architecture and decoration, entertainment, leisure pursuits, diet, dress style, friendships etc......all done with sensitivity to the values the community is based on and the purposes they are driven by. The same applies to profession or trade, financial decisions and wealth building.

Property ownership - we'd need to clarify a good balance of personal/private and corporate property ownership. Every aspect of ownership should be clearly detailed with legal deeds and instruments.

Corporate: Because the community will be on common ground, some of the assets will necessarily be owned, managed and maintained corporately for the common good. For instance, roads, pathways, leisure facilities, farms, etc. Further, services like power, water, sewage, security, laundry, will also have to be provided, owned and managed corporately, for the common good. The value of corporate assets will probably be best held in perpetual trust; with perhaps the possibility of earning dividends or profit-sharing for all the community owners.

Lease or let: the community may also build and let/lease some homes to members who are unable to build or purchase. Terms and tenure, with guarantee, will be formally agreed on a case by case basis.

Personal/Private: individual homes should be owned privately with legal deeds of ownership. Each property may be sold or transferred at the owner's pleasure, at whatever agreed value. However, each sale or transfer must be through the agency of and with the community's consent, to preserve the integrity of community ethos and purpose.

Devotion to one another - devotion to occasions of bible discussion/teaching/study, prayer, worship, eating together and fellowship. Every member and resident should be actively and regularly involved in community gatherings and activities.

Leadership - naturally, both spiritual and administrative leadership will be drawn from the pioneering group, based on their common hearing and understanding of the design and purpose of God for the community; more so if the community is non-denominational or non-affiliated.

However, if the community is part of an established church denomination or movement, leadership may be designated by or in consultation with the movement's primary leaders. In this case, the community would be under the authority of the umbrella church or movement.

Outreach - each community group will develop or evolve outreach systems by which the gospel is intentionally preached to their immediate neighbourhoods and regions - direct or indirect.

The community would host *(public)* gospel/prayer meetings, celebrations, educational and other types of events that non-members may attend, both on community grounds and neutral/regional venues.

Further, as 'salt of the earth' and 'light of the world', the community will develop strategies of preserving, curing, illuminating, transforming and enriching the wider geographical area. Each person will be encouraged, empowered and supported to live a gospel-infused life, preaching the good news in and out of season.

11

Next steps?

We need to, and I strongly urge you, my reader, to head back in the direction of Biblical examples. In the same ways that we seek biblical standards of living on subjects like faith, righteousness, finances, healing, worship, assembly, etc, so we should with community. We should at least head in that direction and by our choices and priorities demonstrate the truth and goodness of sharing a practical common living with fellow believers. We also get to demonstrate to the immediate geographical area that there is a superior and more edifying way to live – a city of light on a hill can not be hidden.

I believe it's really a lot simpler than you might imagine. Below are some 'soft' initial steps that can be taken by anyone; we just need the conviction and courage to begin to do so.

By the way, these do not need to be in antagonism with your denomination, local church or fellowship. It is rather an addition that should complement and strengthen the local church. I am not proposing that churches break up, but rather seek to build communities from their current membership. The larger churches may even be able to more practically facilitate the acquisition of properties through some sort of purchase system.

Intentionally seek out & live around other believers. In the same way some cultures/peoples tend to take over some residential regions or whole towns even, believers (especially of the same persuasion) should be populating some areas. When you are ready to move house, *(or perhaps simply decide to move for this purpose?)* you may as well research where fellow believers might already be living and purposely go and live near them.

Buy or rent together with fellow believers. For instance, with clearly defined ownership and responsibilities, a group of believers could buy a block of flats/apartments; with an agreement to only sell to other affiliated believers when anyone relocates. A group of believers could also decide to self build a residential estate; sourcing and buying land, designing, planning and managing the build and establishing covenants for the possible future sale of any of the units. This will probably work best if all the involved believers belonged to the same church group, however, a group of 'united-purpose same-persuasion' believers could also intentionally instigate such a purchase or development.

Or perhaps you may want to seek out already established communities, interview and interrogate their systems and you just might find one that would receive or suit you the best.

Stop being so scared! Well, at least begin by admitting that

you are scared. But stop being so scared of being, doing, or at least attempting the things you have read that you ought to be and/or do. Begin to actually start trusting the truth that we have been fashioned to "be to the praise of His glory" and that he is "at work in you both to will and to do of his good pleasure", along with all those other verses you like to 'confess' loudly to yourself and just for yourself! Stop being so scared!!

Do something truly scary for a change....for Christ's sake!

12

When?

The Holy Spirit is signifying that the season for change is upon us and as such we should begin to dream, discuss, design, fabricate and invest in the desired future. Begin to mentally untether yourself from your familiar culture and 'normal' life. We must begin to meditate and travail for the birthing of this great kingdom truth as an imperative; incredible transformation awaits.

We must begin to identify our own designated bodies to live true community with, begin to actively challenge and rally support and interest in our circles and then... ....**BEGIN TO LIVE IN COMMUNITY ASAP.**

Another life is possible, potent with power, joy, fulfilment, and the pleasure of God... .... will you dare to explore and live it?

13

Postlude

SHOP IN HEAVEN (adapted from 'Thomas Wingfold, Curate' by George MacDonald: published in 1876)

"Uncle," said Rachel, "may I read your visions of the shops in heaven?"

"Oh no, Rachel. You are not able to read tonight," said her uncle deprecatingly.

"I think I am, uncle. I should like to try. It will let the gentlemen see what you think an ideal state of things should be".

After a little arranging of the sheets, Rachel began. She read not without difficulty, but her pleasure in what she read helped her through.

"And now, said my guide to me, I will bring you to a city of the righteous, and show you how they buy and sell in this 'the kingdom of heaven'. So we journeyed a day and another day and half a day, and I was tired when we arrived there. But when I saw the loveliness of the place, and drew in the healing air thereof, my weariness vanished as a dream of the night, and I said, it is well. I could not now speak of the houses and the dress and the customs of the dwellers therein, but only of what relates to the buying and selling of which I have spoken.

After I had, I know not for how long, refreshed my soul with what it was given me to enjoy; for in all that country there is no such thing as haste, no darting from one thing to another, but a calm eternal progress in which unto the day the good thereof is sufficient. One great afternoon, my guide led me into a large place, such as we would call a shop here, although the arrangements were different, and an air of stateliness dwelt in and around the house. It was filled with the loveliest silken and woollen stuffs, of all kinds and colours, a thousand delights to the eye, and to the thought also, for here was endless harmony, and no discord.

At first, I watched the faces of them that sold; and I could read them because according to the degree of his own capacity, a man there could perfectly read the countenance of every neighbour, that is unless it expressed something that was not in himself, and I could read in them nothing of eagerness, only the calm of a concentrated ministration. There was no seeking there, but strength of giving, a business-like earnestness to supply lack, enlivened by no haste, and dulled by no weariness, brightened ever by the reflected contentment of those who found their wants supplied. As soon as one buyer was contented they turned graciously to another and gave ear until they perfectly understood what object he was seeking. Nor did their countenances change utterly as they turned away, for upon them lingered the satisfaction as of one who hath had a success, and by degrees melted into deep contentment.

Then I turned to watch the countenances of them that bought. And there in like manner, I saw no greed and no meanness. They spake humbly, yet not because they sought a favour, but because they were humble, for their humility was mingled with the confidence of receiving what they sought. And truly it was a pleasure to see how everyone knew what his desire was, making his choice readily and with a decision. I perceived also that everyone spoke not merely respectfully, but gratefully, to him who served him. And at meeting and parting such kindly though brief greetings made me wonder whether every inhabitant of such a mighty city could know every other that dwelt therein. But I soon saw that it came not of individual knowledge, but of universal faith and all-embracing love.

And as I stood and watched, suddenly it came into my mind that I had never yet seen the currency of the country, and therefore I kept my eyes upon a certain woman who bought silk, so that when she paid for the same I might see the money. But the large amount which she bought she took in her arms and carried away, without paying. Therefore I turned to watch another, who bought for a long journey, but when he carried away what he bought, neither did he pay any money. And I said to myself, these must be well-known persons, to whom it is more convenient to pay all at a certain season; and I turned to a third who bought much fine linen. But behold! he paid not. Then I began to observe again those that sold; I thought to myself, how good must be the air of this land for the remembrance of things! for these men write down nothing to keep a record of the moneys men owe them on all sides. And I looked and looked again and yet again, and stood long watching, but so it was throughout the whole place, which thronged and buzzed and swarmed like the busiest of bee-hives; no man paid, and no man had a book in which to write that which the other owed!

Then I turned to my guide and said: How lovely is honesty! and truly from what a labour it absolveth men! for here I see every man keepeth in his mind his own debts, and not the debts of others, so that time is not spent in paying of small sums, neither in the keeping of account of such; but he that buyeth counteth up, and doubtless when the payment day arrives, each comes to pay exactly what is owed, and both are satisfied.

Then my guide smiled, and said, watch yet a while.

And I did as he said unto me, and stood and watched. But the same thing went on everywhere; and I said to myself, Lo, I see nothing new! Suddenly, at my side, a man dropped upon his knees, and bowed his head to the ground. And those that stood near him dropped also upon their knees, and there arose a sound as of soft thunder; and lo! everyone in the place had dropped upon their knees, and spread their hands out before them. Every voice and every noise was hushed, every movement had ceased, and I and my guide alone were left standing.

For certain moments all was utter stillness, every man and woman kneeling, with hands outstretched, save him who had first kneeled, and his hands hung by his sides and his head was still bowed to the earth. After a while, he rose up, and lo! his face was wet with tears; and all the people rose also, and with a noise throughout the place; and the man made a low obeisance to them that were near him, which they returned with equal reverence, and then with downcast eyes he walked slowly from the shop.

The moment he was gone, the business of the place, without a word of remark on any side concerning what had passed, began again and went on as before. People came and went, some more eager and outward, some more staid and inward, but all contented and cheerful. At length, a bell somewhere rang sweet and shrill, and after that no one entered the place, and what was in progress began to be led to a decorous conclusion. In three or four minutes the floor was empty, and the people also of the shop had gone, each about his own affairs, without shutting door or window.

I went out last with my guide, and we seated ourselves under a tree of the willow-kind on the bank of one of the quieter streams, and straightway I began to question him. Tell me, sir, I said, the meaning of what I have seen, for not yet have I understood how these happy people do their business without any money or payments. And he answered, where greed and ambition and self-love rule, money must be: where there is neither greed nor ambition nor self-love, money is needless. And I asked, is it then by the mode of barter that they go about their affairs? Truly I saw no exchange of any sort. My guide said, if thou hadst gone into any other shop throughout the whole city, thou wouldst have seen the same thing. I can't see how that should make the matter clearer to me, I answered. Where neither greed nor ambition nor selfishness reigneth, said my guide, there need and desire have free scope, for they work no evil. But even now I understand you not, sir, I said. Hear me then, answered my guide, for I will speak to you more plainly. Why do men take money in their hands when they go where things are? Because they may not have the things without giving the money. And where they may have things without giving money, do they take money in their hands? Truly no, sir, if there be such a place. Then such a place is this, and so is it here. But how can men give of their goods and receive nothing in return? By receiving everything in return. Tell me, said my guide, why do men take money for their goods? That they may have means to go and buy other things which they need for themselves. But if they also may go to this place or that place where the things they need are, and receive of those things without money and without price, is there then good cause why they should take money in their hands? Truly no, I answered; and I begin, methinks, to see how it works. Yet there are some things I still need to better understand. And first of all, how come men are moved to provide these and those goods for the supply of the wants of their neighbours when they are motivated by no want in themselves, and no advantage to themselves? Thou reasonest, said my guide, as your immature self, who to the eyes of the mature ever look like chrysalids, closed round in a web of their own weaving. Understand that it is never self-advantage that motivates a man in this kingdom to undertake this or that. The only advantage a man derives here is the thing which he doth without thought unto that advantage.

To your world, this world goeth by contraries. The man here that doeth most service, that aideth others the most to the obtaining of their honest desires, is the man who standeth highest with the Lord of the place, and his reward and honour is to be enabled to the spending of himself yet more for the good of his fellows.

Do you think it is a less potent stirring up of thought and energy to desire and seek and find the things that will please the eye, and cheer the brain, and gladden the heart of the people of this great city, so that when one prayeth, 'Give me, friend, of thy loaves,' a man may answer, 'Take of them, friend, as many as thou needest'—is that incentive to diligence less potent than the desire to hoard or to excel? Is it not to share the bliss of God who hoards nothing, but ever giveth liberally?

The joy of a man here is to enable another to lay hold upon that which he needs for life and maturity, and be glad and grow thereby. Strange and unbelievable doctrine to the man in whom the well of life is yet sealed. There are not many in the old world who would enter into the joy of their Lord in this way. Thou knowest, I say, a few in thy world who would willingly consent to be as nothing, so to give life to their fellows. In this city so is it with everyone, in shop or workshop, in study or theatre, all seek to spend and be spent for everyone else. And I said, one thing tell me, sir—how much a man may have for the asking. He answered, whatever he wills, that is, what he can well use. Who then shall be the judge thereof? Who but the man himself? What if he should turn to greed, and begin to hoard and spare? Do you not remember the man earlier, because of whom all business ceased for a time? To that man had come a thought of accumulation instead of growth, and he dropped upon his knees in shame and terror. And thou sawest how all business ceased, and straightway the whole shop turned into what those below call a church; for everyone hastened to the poor man's help, the air was filled with praying breath, and the atmosphere of God-loving souls was around him; the foul thought fled, and the man went forth glad and humble, and tomorrow he will return for that which he needs. If you are present then, you will see him more tenderly ministered unto than all the rest.

But how are men guided as to what to provide for the general good? Every man doeth whatever he can, and the more his labour is desired, the more he rejoices. If a man should desire what he could nowhere find in the city? Then would he straightway do his very best to provide that same thing for all in the city who might after him desire the same. Now, sir, methinks I know and understand, I answered. And we rose and went farther."

"I think that COULD be!" said the curate, breaking the silence that followed when Rachel ceased.

"Not in this world," said the draper.

"To doubt that it COULD be," said the gatekeeper, "would be to doubt whether the kingdom of heaven is a chimaera or a divine idea."

About the Author

Currently a missionary-pastor in North Wales since 2007, I am married to Margaret since 1988 and have two adult children. I am also a Family Mediator, Marriage and Parenting Coach.

I have served as pastor and bible teacher for over 30 years in both denominational and non-denominational settings; I love to see applied biblical principles transform people and circumstances.

I am convinced that Intentional Christian Community living is God's design for Christians and I invite you to come on this incredible journey of transformation, to the glory of God and the multiplied joy of his peoples.

Instagram: @olufemiogunbanwo_gunsbi
  Facebook: olufemi.ogunbanwo

,

Printed in Great Britain
by Amazon

84070171R00058